WORKING PAPERS

Volume II, Chapters 11-19

for use with

FUNDAMENTAL ACCOUNTING PRINCIPLES

Eighth Canadian Edition

Kermit D. Larson
University of Texas-Austin

Morton Nelson
Wilfrid Laurier University

Michael Zin
Professor Emeritus
University of Windsor

Raymond Carroll
Dalhousie University

Represented in Canada by:

McGraw-Hill Ryerson

Toronto • Chicago • Bogotá • Boston • Buenos Aires
Caracas • London • Madrid • Mexico City • Sydney

McGraw-Hill
Ryerson Limited

A Subsidiary of The ***McGraw-Hill*** *Companies*

Printed in the United States of America.

ISBN 0-256-17534-9

2 3 4 5 6 7 8 9 0 VK 3 2 1 0 9 8

Contents

11 Capital Assets: Plant and Equipment 1

12 Capital Assets: Natural Resources, Intangible Assets, and Long-Term Investments 41

13 Current and Long-Term Liabilities 67

14 Partnership Accounting 109

15 Organization and Operation of Corporations 139

16 Additional Corporate Transactions; Reporting Income and Retained Earnings; Earnings Per Share 169

17 Installment Notes Payable and Bonds 195

18 Statement of Changes in Financial Position 243

19 Analyzing Financial Statements 269

CHAPTER 11 EXERCISE 11–1

Name ______________________

EXERCISE 11–2

GENERAL JOURNAL

Page 1

DATE	ACCOUNT TITLES AND EXPLANATION	P.R.	DEBIT	CREDIT

EXERCISE 11–3

GENERAL JOURNAL

Page 1

DATE	ACCOUNT TITLES AND EXPLANATION	P.R.	DEBIT	CREDIT

EXERCISE 11–4

EXERCISE 11–5

Name ____________________

EXERCISE 11–6

CHAPTER 11 EXERCISE 11–7

Part a

Part b

YEAR	BEGINNING BOOK VALUE	ANNUAL AMORTIZATION	ACCUMULATED AMORTIZATION AT THE END OF THE YEAR	ENDING BOOK VALUE

CHAPTER 11 **EXERCISE 11–8** **Name** ______________________

Part a

YEAR	Annual Ammortization

Part b

YEAR	Annual Ammortization

CHAPTER 11 EXERCISE 11–9

GENERAL JOURNAL

Page 1

DATE	ACCOUNT TITLES AND EXPLANATION	P.R.	DEBIT	CREDIT

EXERCISE 11–10

Part a

Part b

GENERAL JOURNAL

Page 2

DATE	ACCOUNT TITLES AND EXPLANATION	P.R.	DEBIT	CREDIT

Part c

Part d

Page 3

DATE	ACCOUNT TITLES AND EXPLANATION	P.R.	DEBIT	CREDIT

 EXERCISE 11–11 **Name** ____________________

GENERAL JOURNAL

Page 1

DATE	ACCOUNT TITLES AND EXPLANATION	P.R.	DEBIT	CREDIT

EXERCISE 11–12

EXERCISE 11–13

GENERAL JOURNAL

Page 1

DATE	ACCOUNT TITLES AND EXPLANATION	P.R.	DEBIT	CREDIT

Name

 Name ____________

Part 1

	LAND	BUILDING	BUILDING	LAND IMPROVEMENTS	LAND IMPROVEMENTS

Parts 2 and 3

GENERAL JOURNAL

Page 1

DATE	ACCOUNT TITLES AND EXPLANATION	P.R.	DEBIT	CREDIT

CHAPTER 11 PROBLEM 11–2 Name ____________

Part 1

GENERAL JOURNAL **Page 1**

DATE	ACCOUNT TITLES AND EXPLANATION	P.R.	DEBIT	CREDIT

Part 2

Parts 3. and 4

 Name ____________

Part 1

YEAR	STRAIGHT LINE	UNITS OF PRODUCTION	DECLINING BALANCE
TOTALS			

CHAPTER 11 PROBLEM 11–3 (Concluded)
Part 2

GENERAL JOURNAL

Page 1

DATE	ACCOUNT TITLES AND EXPLANATION	P.R.	DEBIT	CREDIT

 Name ______________

GENERAL JOURNAL Page 1

DATE	ACCOUNT TITLES AND EXPLANATION	P.R.	DEBIT	CREDIT

Page 2

DATE	ACCOUNT TITLES AND EXPLANATION	P.R.	DEBIT	CREDIT

 Name ____________

GENERAL JOURNAL Page 1

DATE	ACCOUNT TITLES AND EXPLANATION	P.R.	DEBIT	CREDIT

Page 2

DATE	ACCOUNT TITLES AND EXPLANATION	P.R.	DEBIT	CREDIT

 Name ______________

GENERAL JOURNAL Page 1

DATE	ACCOUNT TITLES AND EXPLANATION	P.R.	DEBIT	CREDIT

Page 2

DATE	ACCOUNT TITLES AND EXPLANATION	P.R.	DEBIT	CREDIT

Name ______________________

Name ____________________

Part 1

YEAR	STRAIGHT LINE	UNITS OF PRODUCTION	DECLINING BALANCE
TOTALS			

Part 2

GENERAL JOURNAL

Page 1

DATE	ACCOUNT TITLES AND EXPLANATION	P.R.	DEBIT	CREDIT

 Name ____________________

DATE	EXPLANATION	P.R.	DEBIT	CREDIT	BALANCE

Name ____________________

Part 1

	LAND	BUILDING	BUILDING	LAND IMPROVEMENTS	LAND IMPROVEMENTS

Parts 2 and 3

GENERAL JOURNAL Page 1

DATE	ACCOUNT TITLES AND EXPLANATION	P.R.	DEBIT	CREDIT

 Name ______________________

Part 1

GENERAL JOURNAL Page 1

DATE	ACCOUNT TITLES AND EXPLANATION	P.R.	DEBIT	CREDIT

Part 2

Part 3

Part 4

YEAR	(A) ANNUAL AMORTIZATION EXPENSE	BEGINNING BOOK VALUE	(B) ANNUAL AMORTIZATION EXPENSE	REMAINING BOOK VALUE

Name ______________

Part 2

GENERAL JOURNAL

Page 1

DATE	ACCOUNT TITLES AND EXPLANATION	P.R.	DEBIT	CREDIT

 Name ______________________

 Name ____________________

CHAPTER 12 EXERCISE 12–1 Name ____________

GENERAL JOURNAL Page 1

DATE	ACCOUNT TITLES AND EXPLANATION	P.R.	DEBIT	CREDIT

EXERCISE 12–2

GENERAL JOURNAL Page 1

DATE	ACCOUNT TITLES AND EXPLANATION	P.R.	DEBIT	CREDIT

CHAPTER 12 EXERCISE 12–3

EXERCISE 12–4

Name ______________________

GENERAL JOURNAL

Page 1

DATE	ACCOUNT TITLES AND EXPLANATION	P.R.	DEBIT	CREDIT

 Name ______________________

CHAPTER 12 EXERCISE 12–8

GENERAL JOURNAL

Page 1

DATE	ACCOUNT TITLES AND EXPLANATION	P.R.	DEBIT	CREDIT

EXERCISE 12–9

CHAPTER 12 PROBLEM 12–1 Name ______________________

Part 1

GENERAL JOURNAL Page 1

DATE	ACCOUNT TITLES AND EXPLANATION	P.R.	DEBIT	CREDIT

Part 2

GENERAL JOURNAL Page 2

DATE	ACCOUNT TITLES AND EXPLANATION	P.R.	DEBIT	CREDIT

 Name ______________

Name ____________________

Part 1

GENERAL JOURNAL

Page 1

DATE	ACCOUNT TITLES AND EXPLANATION	P.R.	DEBIT	CREDIT

Name

Part 1

Part 2

GENERAL JOURNAL

Page 1

DATE	ACCOUNT TITLES AND EXPLANATION	P.R.	DEBIT	CREDIT

Part 3

 Name ____________

Part 1

GENERAL JOURNAL Page 1

DATE	ACCOUNT TITLES AND EXPLANATION	P.R.	DEBIT	CREDIT

GENERAL JOURNAL

Page 2

DATE	ACCOUNT TITLES AND EXPLANATION	P.R.	DEBIT	CREDIT

Parts 2 and 3

 Name ______________

Part 3

 Name ____________________

Page 2

DATE	ACCOUNT TITLES AND EXPLANATION	P.R.	DEBIT	CREDIT

Name ______________________

Page 2

DATE	ACCOUNT TITLES AND EXPLANATION	P.R.	DEBIT	CREDIT

Name ______________________

Page 2

DATE	ACCOUNT TITLES AND EXPLANATION	P.R.	DEBIT	CREDIT

CHAPTER 13 EXERCISE 13–1 Name ____________

EXERCISE 13–2

GENERAL JOURNAL Page 1

DATE	ACCOUNT TITLES AND EXPLANATION	P.R.	DEBIT	CREDIT

 EXERCISE 13–3

GENERAL JOURNAL

Page 1

DATE	ACCOUNT TITLES AND EXPLANATION	P.R.	DEBIT	CREDIT

 Name ______________

GENERAL JOURNAL Page 1

DATE	ACCOUNT TITLES AND EXPLANATION	P.R.	DEBIT	CREDIT

CHAPTER 13 EXERCISE 13–5

GENERAL JOURNAL

Page 1

DATE	ACCOUNT TITLES AND EXPLANATION	P.R.	DEBIT	CREDIT

 EXERCISE 13–6 Name ____________

EXERCISE 13–7

Name ______________________

GENERAL JOURNAL

Page 1

DATE	ACCOUNT TITLES AND EXPLANATION	P.R.	DEBIT	CREDIT

Name ____________________

Parts a and b

Part c and d

GENERAL JOURNAL

Page 1

DATE	ACCOUNT TITLES AND EXPLANATION	P.R.	DEBIT	CREDIT

Name

 Name ____________________

Parts 1 - 4

Part 5

GENERAL JOURNAL Page 1

DATE	ACCOUNT TITLES AND EXPLANATION	P.R.	DEBIT	CREDIT

Part 5

GENERAL JOURNAL

Page 1

DATE	ACCOUNT TITLES AND EXPLANATION	P.R.	DEBIT	CREDIT

 Name ____________

Part 1

Part 2

GENERAL JOURNAL Page 1

DATE	ACCOUNT TITLES AND EXPLANATION	P.R.	DEBIT	CREDIT

CHAPTER 13 PROBLEM 13–3 (Concluded)

Parts 3 and 4

CHAPTER 13 PROBLEM 13–4 Name ____________________

Part 1

Part 2

Part 3

Part 4

GENERAL JOURNAL Page

DATE	ACCOUNT TITLES AND EXPLANATION	P.R.	DEBIT	CREDIT

Part 5

 Name ______________

Parts 1 and 2

Parts 3 - 8

Part 9

 Name ____________

Part 1

GENERAL JOURNAL

Page 1

DATE	ACCOUNT TITLES AND EXPLANATION	P.R.	DEBIT	CREDIT

Part 2

GENERAL JOURNAL

Page 2

DATE	ACCOUNT TITLES AND EXPLANATION	P.R.	DEBIT	CREDIT

 Name ____________

GENERAL JOURNAL Page 1

DATE	ACCOUNT TITLES AND EXPLANATION	P.R.	DEBIT	CREDIT

Page 2

DATE	ACCOUNT TITLES AND EXPLANATION	P.R.	DEBIT	CREDIT

 Name ______

CHAPTER 13 PROBLEM 13–9 Name ____________________

Part 1

Part 2

YEAR	(a) FACE AMOUNT OF NOTE	(b) UNAMORTIZED DISCOUNT AT BEGINNING OF YEAR	(c) BEGINNING NET LIABILITY (a) – (b)	(d) DISCOUNT TO BE AMORTIZED (c) × ______%	(e) UNAMORTIZED DISCOUNT AT THE END OF YEAR (b) – (d)	(f) ENDING NET LIABILITY (a) – (e)

Part 3

GENERAL JOURNAL Page 1

DATE	ACCOUNT TITLES AND EXPLANATION	P.R.	DEBIT	CREDIT

Part 4

Part 1

Part 2

YEAR	(a) BEGINNING GROSS LEASE LIABILITY	(b) UNAMORTIZED DISCOUNT AT BEGINNING OF YEAR	(c) BEGINNING NET LIABILITY (a) − (b)	(d) DISCOUNT TO BE AMORTIZED (c) × ____%	(e) UNAMORTIZED DISCOUNT AT THE END OF YEAR (b) − (d)	(f) ENDING GROSS NET LIABILITY (a) − $____	(g) ENDING NET LIABILITY (f) − (e)

Part 3

GENERAL JOURNAL — Page 1

DATE	ACCOUNT TITLES AND EXPLANATION	P.R.	DEBIT	CREDIT

Part 4

GENERAL JOURNAL

Page 2

DATE	ACCOUNT TITLES AND EXPLANATION	P.R.	DEBIT	CREDIT

Parts 5 and 6

GENERAL JOURNAL

Page 3

DATE	ACCOUNT TITLES AND EXPLANATION	P.R.	DEBIT	CREDIT

COMPREHENSIVE PROBLEM
Schwartz Exterminator Company
Part 1

Name ______________________

COMPREHENSIVE PROBLEM
Schwartz Exterminator Company (Continued)

Name ______________________

COMPREHENSIVE PROBLEM
Schwartz Exterminator Company (Continued)
Part 2

SCHWARTZ EXTERMINATOR COMPANY

Six-Column Table

For Year Ended December 31, 1996

ACCOUNT TITLES	UNADJUSTED TRIAL BALANCE		ADJUSTMENTS		ADJUSTED TRIAL BALANCE	
	DR.	CR.	DR.	CR.	DR.	CR.
Cash						
Accounts receivable						
Allowance for doubtful accounts						
Merchandise inventory						
Trucks						
Accumulated depreciation, trucks						
Equipment						
Accumulated depreciation, equip.						
Accounts payable						
Estimated warranty liability						
Unearned exterm. serv. revenue						
Long-term notes payable						
Discount on notes payable						
Arnold Schwartz, capital						
Arnold Schwartz, withdrawals						
Extermination services revenue						
Interest earned						
Sales						
Purchases						
Depreciation expense, trucks						
Depreciation expense, equip.						
Wages expense						
Interest expense						
Rent expense						
Bad debts expense						
Miscellaneous expenses						
Repairs expense						
Utilities expense						
Warranty expense						

COMPREHENSIVE PROBLEM

Name ____________________

Schwartz Exterminator Company (Continued)

Part 3

GENERAL JOURNAL

Page 2

DATE	ACCOUNT TITLES AND EXPLANATION	P.R.	DEBIT	CREDIT

COMPREHENSIVE PROBLEM
Schwartz Exterminator Company (Continued)
Part 4

SCHWARTZ EXTERMINATOR COMPANY

Income Statement

For Year Ended December 31, 1996

SCHWARTZ EXTERMINATOR COMPANY

Statement of Changes in Owner's Equity

For Year Ended December 31, 1996

Name ____________________

SCHWARTZ EXTERMINATOR COMPANY

Balance Sheet

December 31, 1996

 Name ______________

GENERAL JOURNAL Page 1

DATE	ACCOUNT TITLES AND EXPLANATION	P.R.	DEBIT	CREDIT

EXERCISE 14–2

EXERCISE 14–3

CHAPTER 14 EXERCISE 14–4

Name ____________________

GENERAL JOURNAL

Page 1

DATE	ACCOUNT TITLES AND EXPLANATION	P.R.	DEBIT	CREDIT

EXERCISE 14–5

GENERAL JOURNAL

Page 1

DATE	ACCOUNT TITLES AND EXPLANATION	P.R.	DEBIT	CREDIT

CHAPTER 14 EXERCISE 14-6

GENERAL JOURNAL Page 1

DATE	ACCOUNT TITLES AND EXPLANATION	P.R.	DEBIT	CREDIT

EXERCISE 14-7
Part 1

Parts 2 and 3

GENERAL JOURNAL Page 1

DATE	ACCOUNT TITLES AND EXPLANATION	P.R.	DEBIT	CREDIT

 Name ____________

 EXERCISE 14-9

 Name ____________________

DATE	ACCOUNT TITLES AND EXPLANATION	P.R.	DEBIT	CREDIT

 Name ____________________

Inc./Loss Sharing Plan	Year __________ *Calculations*		

Inc./Loss Sharing Plan	Year ____________ *Calculations*		

Inc./Loss Sharing Plan	Year ____________ *Calculations*		

 Name ____________

Inc./Loss Sharing Plan	Year ____________ Calculations		

Inc./Loss Sharing Plan	Year ____________ Calculations		

Inc./Loss Sharing Plan	Year ________ Calculations		

 Name ____________________

Part 1

Inc./Loss Sharing Plan	Calculations				

Part 2

 Name ______________________

DATE	ACCOUNT TITLES AND EXPLANATION	P.R.	DEBIT	CREDIT

Name ______________________

Part 1

Inc./Loss Sharing Plan	Calculations				

Part 2

 Name ______________________

Part 3

DATE	ACCOUNT TITLES AND EXPLANATION	P.R.	DEBIT	CREDIT

Name ____________________

GENERAL JOURNAL

DATE	ACCOUNT TITLES AND EXPLANATION	P.R.	DEBIT	CREDIT

DATE	ACCOUNT TITLES AND EXPLANATION	P.R.	DEBIT	CREDIT

 Name ______________

GENERAL JOURNAL

DATE	ACCOUNT TITLES AND EXPLANATION	P.R.	DEBIT	CREDIT

GENERAL JOURNAL

DATE	ACCOUNT TITLES AND EXPLANATION	P.R.	DEBIT	CREDIT

 Name ____________

GENERAL JOURNAL

DATE	ACCOUNT TITLES AND EXPLANATION	P.R.	DEBIT	CREDIT

GENERAL JOURNAL

DATE	ACCOUNT TITLES AND EXPLANATION	P.R.	DEBIT	CREDIT

 Name ____________

GENERAL JOURNAL Page 1

DATE	ACCOUNT TITLES AND EXPLANATION	P.R.	DEBIT	CREDIT

GENERAL JOURNAL

Page 1

DATE	ACCOUNT TITLES AND EXPLANATION	P.R.	DEBIT	CREDIT

 EXERCISE 15–3

Name ______________________

GENERAL JOURNAL

Page 1

DATE	ACCOUNT TITLES AND EXPLANATION	P.R.	DEBIT	CREDIT

EXERCISE 15–4

GENERAL JOURNAL

Page 1

DATE	ACCOUNT TITLES AND EXPLANATION	P.R.	DEBIT	CREDIT

EXERCISE 15–5

EXERCISE 15–6

 Name ______________________

EXERCISE 15–8

EXERCISE 15–9

GENERAL JOURNAL

Page 1

DATE	ACCOUNT TITLES AND EXPLANATION	P.R.	DEBIT	CREDIT

Name ______________________

CHAPTER 15 PROBLEM 15–1 Name ____________________

Part 1

GENERAL JOURNAL Page 1

DATE	ACCOUNT TITLES AND EXPLANATION	P.R.	DEBIT	CREDIT

Page 2

DATE	ACCOUNT TITLES AND EXPLANATION	P.R.	DEBIT	CREDIT

Part 2

Name ____________________

Part 1

GENERAL JOURNAL

Page 1

DATE	ACCOUNT TITLES AND EXPLANATION	P.R.	DEBIT	CREDIT

 PROBLEM 15–2 (Concluded)

Page 2

DATE	ACCOUNT TITLES AND EXPLANATION	P.R.	DEBIT	CREDIT

Part 2

 Name ______________

Part 1

GENERAL JOURNAL

Page 1

DATE	ACCOUNT TITLES AND EXPLANATION	P.R.	DEBIT	CREDIT

DATE	ACCOUNT TITLES AND EXPLANATION	P.R.	DEBIT	CREDIT

Part 2

CHAPTER 15 PROBLEM 15–4 Name ____________

Part 1

 PROBLEM 15–4 (Continued)

Part 2

(a) Preferred is noncumulative

YEAR	CALCULATIONS	PREFERRED DIVIDEND PER SHARE	COMMON DIVIDEND PER SHARE

(b) Preferred is cumulative

YEAR	CALCULATIONS	PREFERRED DIVIDEND PER SHARE	COMMON DIVIDEND PER SHARE

 Name ____________________

(c) Preferred is noncumulative

YEAR	CALCULATIONS	PREFERRED DIVIDEND PER SHARE	COMMON DIVIDEND PER SHARE

(b) Preferred is cumulative

YEAR	CALCULATIONS	PREFERRED DIVIDEND PER SHARE	COMMON DIVIDEND PER SHARE

CHAPTER 15 **PROBLEM 15–5** **Name** ______________________

Part 1

Part 2

(a) Preferred is noncumulative

YEAR	CALCULATIONS	PREFERRED DIVIDEND PER SHARE	COMMON DIVIDEND PER SHARE

(b) Preferred is cumulative

YEAR	CALCULATIONS	PREFERRED DIVIDEND PER SHARE	COMMON DIVIDEND PER SHARE

 Name ______________________

(c) Preferred is noncumulative

YEAR	CALCULATIONS	PREFERRED DIVIDEND PER SHARE	COMMON DIVIDEND PER SHARE

(b) Preferred is cumulative

YEAR	CALCULATIONS	PREFERRED DIVIDEND PER SHARE	COMMON DIVIDEND PER SHARE

Name ____________________

1) The market value of a common share is $____________________.

2) The book value of a preferred share is $____________________ and the book value of a common share is $____________________.

3) The book value of a preferred share is $____________________ and the book value of a common share is $____________________.

Name ______________________

 Name ______________________

EXERCISE 16–1

Name ____________________

Part 1

GENERAL JOURNAL — Page 1

DATE	ACCOUNT TITLES AND EXPLANATION	P.R.	DEBIT	CREDIT

Part 2

EXERCISE 16–2

Parts 1 and 2

CHAPTER 16 EXERCISE 16-3

GENERAL JOURNAL

Page 1

DATE	ACCOUNT TITLES AND EXPLANATION	P.R.	DEBIT	CREDIT

EXERCISE 16-4

GENERAL JOURNAL

Page 1

DATE	ACCOUNT TITLES AND EXPLANATION	P.R.	DEBIT	CREDIT

 EXERCISE 16–5 Name ______________________

EXERCISE 16–6

EXERCISE 16-7

TIME PERIOD	SHARES OUTSTANDING ADJUSTED FOR STOCK DIVIDEND OR SPLIT	PORTION OF YEAR	

EXERCISE 16-8

TIME PERIOD	SHARES OUTSTANDING ADJUSTED FOR STOCK DIVIDEND OR SPLIT	PORTION OF YEAR	

 Name ________________

Name

Name ____________________

Part 1

GENERAL JOURNAL

Page 1

DATE	ACCOUNT TITLES AND EXPLANATION	P.R.	DEBIT	CREDIT

Part 2

Part 3

Name ______________________

 Name ____________________

CHAPTER 16 PROBLEM 16–5 Name ____________________

Part 1

Part 2

YEAR	AMORTIZATION		AMORTIZATION

Part 3

Part 4

Part 1

Name ____________________

TIME PERIOD	SHARES OUTSTANDING ADJUSTED FOR STOCK DIVIDEND OR SPLIT	PORTION OF YEAR	

Part 2

Part 4

Name ______________________

Name ______________________

GENERAL JOURNAL

Page 1

DATE	ACCOUNT TITLES AND EXPLANATION	P.R.	DEBIT	CREDIT

GENERAL JOURNAL

Page 1

DATE	ACCOUNT TITLES AND EXPLANATION	P.R.	DEBIT	CREDIT

 Name ____________________

GENERAL JOURNAL Page 1

DATE	ACCOUNT TITLES AND EXPLANATION	P.R.	DEBIT	CREDIT

EXERCISE 17–6

GENERAL JOURNAL

Page 1

DATE	ACCOUNT TITLES AND EXPLANATION	P.R.	DEBIT	CREDIT

 EXERCISE 17–7 Name ____________

GENERAL JOURNAL Page 1

DATE	ACCOUNT TITLES AND EXPLANATION	P.R.	DEBIT	CREDIT

Name ______________________

GENERAL JOURNAL

Page 1

DATE	ACCOUNT TITLES AND EXPLANATION	P.R.	DEBIT	CREDIT

Name ______________________

Name ____________________

GENERAL JOURNAL

Page 1

DATE	ACCOUNT TITLES AND EXPLANATION	P.R.	DEBIT	CREDIT

 Name ____________________

GENERAL JOURNAL

Page 1

DATE	ACCOUNT TITLES AND EXPLANATION	P.R.	DEBIT	CREDIT

CHAPTER 17 PROBLEM 17–1 Name ____________________

Parts 1, 2 and 3

GENERAL JOURNAL Page 1

DATE	ACCOUNT TITLES AND EXPLANATION	P.R.	DEBIT	CREDIT

Part 4

GENERAL JOURNAL Page 1

DATE	ACCOUNT TITLES AND EXPLANATION	P.R.	DEBIT	CREDIT

 Name ____________

Parts 1, 2 and 3

GENERAL JOURNAL Page 1

DATE	ACCOUNT TITLES AND EXPLANATION	P.R.	DEBIT	CREDIT

CHAPTER 17 PROBLEM 17–3 Name ______________

Part 1

GENERAL JOURNAL Page 1

DATE	ACCOUNT TITLES AND EXPLANATION	P.R.	DEBIT	CREDIT

Part 2

Part 3

Part 4

Part 5

GENERAL JOURNAL

Page 1

DATE	ACCOUNT TITLES AND EXPLANATION	P.R.	DEBIT	CREDIT

CHAPTER 17 PROBLEM 17–4 Name ______________

Part 1

GENERAL JOURNAL

Page 1

DATE	ACCOUNT TITLES AND EXPLANATION	P.R.	DEBIT	CREDIT

Part 2

Part 3

Part 4

Part 5

GENERAL JOURNAL

Page 1

DATE	ACCOUNT TITLES AND EXPLANATION	P.R.	DEBIT	CREDIT

CHAPTER 17 PROBLEM 17–5 Name ______________

Part 1

GENERAL JOURNAL Page 1

DATE	ACCOUNT TITLES AND EXPLANATION	P.R.	DEBIT	CREDIT

Part 2

Part 3

Part 4

Parts 5 and 6

GENERAL JOURNAL

Page 1

DATE	ACCOUNT TITLES AND EXPLANATION	P.R.	DEBIT	CREDIT

Name ____________________

Part 2

GENERAL JOURNAL

Page 1

DATE	ACCOUNT TITLES AND EXPLANATION	P.R.	DEBIT	CREDIT

Part 3

Name

 Name ____________

Part 1

____

____

____

____

____

____

____

____

____

____

Part 2

PERIOD ENDING	(a) BEGINNING PRINCIPAL BALANCE	(b) PERIODIC PAYMENT	(c) INTEREST EXPENSE FOR THE PERIOD (a) × ______%	(d) PORTION OF PAYMENT THAT IS PRINCIPAL (b) − (c)	(e) ENDING PRINCIPAL BALANCE (a) − (d)

Part 3

GENERAL JOURNAL Page 1

DATE	ACCOUNT TITLES AND EXPLANATION	P.R.	DEBIT	CREDIT

Part 4

GENERAL JOURNAL

Page 2

DATE	ACCOUNT TITLES AND EXPLANATION	P.R.	DEBIT	CREDIT

CHAPTER 17 PROBLEM 17–10 Name ______________________

Part 1

Part 2

PERIOD ENDING	(a) BEGINNING CARRYING AMOUNT	(b) INTEREST EXPENSE FOR THE PERIOD	(c) INTEREST TO BE PAID THE BONDHOLDERS	(d) ______ TO BE AMORTIZED	(e) UNAMORTIZED ______ AT END OF PERIOD	(f) ENDING CARRYING AMOUNT

Part 3

GENERAL JOURNAL Page 1

DATE	ACCOUNT TITLES AND EXPLANATION	P.R.	DEBIT	CREDIT

 Name ____________________

Part 1

Part 2

PERIOD ENDING	(a) BEGINNING CARRYING AMOUNT	(b) INTEREST EXPENSE FOR THE PERIOD	(c) INTEREST TO BE PAID THE BONDHOLDERS	(d) ______ TO BE AMORTIZED	(e) UNAMORTIZED ______ AT END OF PERIOD	(f) ENDING CARRYING AMOUNT

Part 3

GENERAL JOURNAL Page 1

DATE	ACCOUNT TITLES AND EXPLANATION	P.R.	DEBIT	CREDIT

 Name ____________________

PERIOD ENDING	(a) BEGINNING CARRYING AMOUNT	(b) INTEREST EXPENSE FOR THE PERIOD	(c) INTEREST TO BE PAID THE BONDHOLDERS	(d) ______ TO BE AMORTIZED	(e) UNAMORTIZED ______ AT END OF PERIOD	(f) ENDING CARRYING AMOUNT

GENERAL JOURNAL Page 1

DATE	ACCOUNT TITLES AND EXPLANATION	P.R.	DEBIT	CREDIT

CHAPTER 17 PROBLEM 17–13 Name ______________________

Parts 1–3

GENERAL JOURNAL Page 1

DATE	ACCOUNT TITLES AND EXPLANATION	P.R.	DEBIT	CREDIT

Part 4

	INTEREST-METHOD AMORTIZATION			STRAIGHT-LINE AMORTIZATION		
PERIOD ENDING	BEGINNING-OF-PERIOD CARRYING AMOUNT	INTEREST EXPENSE TO BE RECORDED	INTEREST EXPENSE AS A % OF CARRYING AMOUNT	BEGINNING-OF-PERIOD CARRYING AMOUNT	INTEREST EXPENSE TO BE RECORDED	INTEREST EXPENSE AS A % OF CARRYING AMOUNT

GENERAL JOURNAL

DATE	ACCOUNT TITLES AND EXPLANATION	P.R.	DEBIT	CREDIT

Name ______________________

 Name ______________________

CHAPTER 18 EXERCISE 18–1 **Name** ______________________

	STATEMENT OF CHANGES IN FINANCIAL POSITION		
	OPERATING ACTIVITIES	INVESTING ACTIVITIES	FINANCING ACTIVITIES
a. Long-term bonds payable were retired by issuing common stock.			
b. Surplus merchandise inventory was sold for cash.			
c. Borrowed cash from the bank by signing a nine-month note payable.			
d. Paid cash to purchase a patent.			
e. A six-month note receivable was accepted in exchange for a building that had been used in operations.			
f. Recorded depreciation expense on all plant assets.			
g. A cash dividend that had been declared in a previous period was paid in the current period.			

CHAPTER 18 EXERCISE 18–2

 EXERCISE 18–3 Name ____________________

EXERCISE 18–4

 EXERCISE 18–5 Name ____________

EXERCISE 18–6

 Name ____________________

	STATEMENT OF CHANGES IN FINANCIAL POSITION		
	OPERATING ACTIVITIES	INVESTING ACTIVITIES	FINANCING ACTIVITIES
a. Land for a new plant was purchased by issuing common shares.			
b. Recorded amortization expense.			
c. Income taxes payable increased by 15% from prior year.			
d. Declared and paid a cash dividend.			
e. Merchandise inventory increased.			
f. Sold plant equipment at a loss.			
g. Accounts receivable decreased during the year.			

			ANALYSIS OF CHANGES		
			DEBIT	CREDIT	

			ANALYSIS OF CHANGES		
			DEBIT	CREDIT	

 Name ______________________

Name ______________________

			ANALYSIS OF CHANGES		
			DEBIT	CREDIT	

			ANALYSIS OF CHANGES		
			DEBIT	CREDIT	

 Name ____________________

Name ____________________

 Name ____________________

Part a

Part b

Part c

 Name ____________________

			ANALYSIS OF CHANGES		
			DEBIT	CREDIT	

 PROBLEM 18–7 (Concluded)

			ANALYSIS OF CHANGES		
			DEBIT	CREDIT	

 Name ____________________

Name ______________________

 EXERCISE 19–1

Name ______________________

EXERCISE 19–2

 EXERCISE 19–3

EXERCISE 19–4

 Name

EXERCISE 19–8

EXERCISE 19–9

 Name ____________

Part 1

Part 2

Part 3

Part 4

CHAPTER 19 PROBLEM 19–2 Name ____________________

Part 1

Income Statement Trends for Years Ended December 31, 19X7-X1

	19X7	19X6	19X5	19X4	19X3	19X2	19X1
Sales							100.0
Cost of goods sold							100.0
Gross profit from sales							100.0
Operating expenses							100.0
Income before taxes							100.0

Balance sheet Trends, December 31, 19X7-X1

	19X7	19X6	19X5	19X4	19X3	19X2	19X1
Cash							100.0
Accounts receivable, net							100.0
Merchandise inventory							100.0
Other current assets							100.0
Long-term investments							100.0
Plant and equipment, net							100.0
Total assets							100.0
Current liabilities							100.0
Long-term liabilities							100.0
Common stock							100.0
Other contributed capital							100.0
Retained earnings							100.0

Part 2

 Name

 Name ______________

Part 1

Part 2

CHAPTER 19 PROBLEM 19–5

Name ____________________

Name ______________________

Part 1

Part 2

Part 3

Part 4

CHAPTER 19 PROBLEM 19–7 Name ______________________

Part 1

Income Statement Trends for Years Ended December 31, 1996-90

	1996	1995	1994	1993	1992	1991	1990
Sales							100.0
Cost of goods sold							100.0
Gross profit from sales							100.0
Operating expenses							100.0
Income before taxes							100.0

Balance sheet Trends, December 31, 1996-90

	1996	1995	1994	1993	1992	1991	1990
Cash							100.0
Accounts receivable, net							100.0
Merchandise inventory							100.0
Other current assets							100.0
Long-term investments							100.0
Plant assets, net							100.0
Total assets							100.0
Current liabilities							100.0
Long-term liabilities							100.0
Common share capital							100.0
Retained earnings							100.0

Part 2

Name ____________________

Name ____________________

Parts 1 and 2

 Name ____________________

TRANSACTION	CURRENT RATIO	ACID-TEST RATIO	WORKING CAPITAL

Notes

Notes